IKEBANA with
Living Plants

IKEBANA with Living Plants

Ichiba Ashida

Shufunotomo / Japan Publications

First printing, 1998

© Copyright in Japan 1998 by Ichiba Ashida
Photographs by Akira Takahashi, Gesho Ogura
English text: translated by Kimiko Steiner, supervised by Jane Singer
Book design by Momoyo Nishimura

Published by Shufunotomo Co., Ltd.
2-9, Kanda Surugadai, Chiyoda-ku, Tokyo, 101-8911 Japan

DISTRIBUTORS
United States: Kodansha America, Inc., through Oxford University Press,
199 Madison Avenue, New York, NY 10016.
Canada: Fitzhenry & Whiteside Ltd.,
195 Allstate Parkway, Markham, Ontario L3R 4T8.
United Kingdom and Europe: Premier Book Marketing Ltd.,
1 Gower Street, London WC1E 6HA.
Australia and New Zealand: Bookwise International,
54 Crittenden Road, Findon, South Australia 5023.
The Far East and Japan: Japan Publications Trading Co., Ltd.,
1-2-1, Sarugaku-cho, Chiyoda-ku, Tokyo 101, Japan

ISBN: 0-87040-903-4
Printed in Japan

CONTENTS

PREFACE

Ikebana with Living Plants is our name for a totally new type of flower arrangement using potted plants and cut flowers of the season. By incorporating cut flowers with a potted plant you create a completely new ambiance, giving the plant a fresh new look. You can enjoy many different variations in your arrangements, although all of the styles are based on the basic trifold ikebana form of Heaven, Earth and Man. Ikebana with Living Plants is perfectly suited to our modern lifestyles: With the simple addition of cut materials, you can beautify gifts of potted plants, enliven the atmosphere at parties and for home entertaining, and enhance your interior decor, enriching your life throughout the four seasons.

With Ikebana with Living Plants you not only improve your surroundings, but you add appeal to your daily life by creating beauty with these unique combinations of flowers and plants.

Ichiba Ashida

The Eight Types of Potted Plants

You can choose from a wide variety of potted plants in gardening stores and florist shops. The selection is nearly limitless, from flowering grasses to flowering trees to leafy plants, but they can all be classified into four main types of plants — four flowering plants and four leafy plants.

FLOWERS

I. Tall potted flowers:

With erect stems and flowers blooming at a high position.

Examples:
Cattleya orchid
Chinese lantern (*Physalis alkekengi*)
Coralberry (*Ardisia crenata*)
Freesia
Fuchsia
Jasmine (*Stephanotis floribunda*)
Sasanqua camellia
Tulip

II. Upright, long-stemmed potted flowers:

With long-stemmed flowers and low leaves.

Examples:
Cyclamen
Geranium
Kalanchoe
Marguerite
Paphiopedilum

III. Densely blooming potted flowers:
The densely growing flowers and leaves form a solid mass.

Examples:
Begonia semperflorens
Bougainvillea
Carnation
Chinese chili pepper (*Capsicum annum*)
Chrysanthemum
Cineraria
Clematis
Daisy
Gardenia
Hydrangea
Pelargonium
Petunia
Poinsettia
Pomegranate
Prairie gentian
Rhododendron
Saintpaulia
Zinnia *elegans*

IV. Low, compact-bodied potted flowers:
With low leaves and short-stemmed flowers blooming at a low position.

Examples:
Ageratum
Aster
Begonia flamingo
Cactus (*schlumbergera*)
Chinese chili pepper (*Capsicum annum*)
Marigold

LEAFY PLANTS

V. Tall, leafy potted plants:

The body of the plant extends to some height but the leaves are not dense.

Examples:
Anthurium
Capoc
Croton
Dracaena corderine 'crystal'
Dracaena godseffina
Ficus benjamina (Benjamin tree)
Palm

VI. Densely growing leafy potted plants:

With a full, rounded shape and densely growing leaves.

Examples:
Ananas
Asparagus
Boston fern
Caladium
Calathea
Dieffenbachia
Dracaena sanderiana
Kochia scoparia
Maidenhair fern (*Adiantum*)
Maranta
Monstera
Morning glory

VII. Potted plants with low, compact leaves:
The leaves form a low, dense mass.

Examples:
Coleus
Dracaena
Basket plant (*Aeschynanthus*)
Fitnia
Flowering cabbage (*Brassica oleracea*)
Geranium
Poinsettia

VIII. Potted plants with dangling stems:
With dangling flowers and stems.

Examples:
Cat-tail
Chlorophytum comosum
Basket plant (*Aeschynanthus*)
Green necklace
Ivy
Pepperomia sandercie
Philodendron selloum
Pothos
Spiderwort (*Tradescantia*)

Using Flower Holders and Other Tools

Unlike traditional flower arrangements, flower pot arrangements do not use vases or other containers holding water. Instead, cut flowers are set into the soil of the flower pot. Naturally, if we placed the flower stems directly into the soil, they would soon wither, so we have developed a set of special flower containers (see photo). The flower holder, or *kenzutsu*, is a cone-shaped water holder in which you place a *kenzan* (spiked metal stand) and add water. After you insert the cut flowers, set the flower holder into the soil of the potted plant.

When you want to place cut flowers at a high position in the potted plant, you can attach the coated metal skewers, included in the flower holder set, to the base of the flower holders to adjust their height. There are five sizes of flower holders: large, middle, small, mini and extra-mini, and there are three sizes of *kenzan*: one each for the large, middle and small flower holders (you need not use *kenzan* with the mini or extra-mini flower holders).

Part 1

Arrangements in Living Spaces

Materials:
Potted plant: Boston fern
Cut flowers: Gerbera, Thunberg's spirea, *Dendrobium phalaenopsis*
Outer container: Ceramic pot

14

You can create a lovely gift by adding some cut flowers to potted plants and placing them in attractive containers.
[Left]
Materials:
Potted plants: Calathea, *Philodendron selloum*, palm
Cut flowers: Freesia, camellia **Outer container:** Wooden cask

16

[Right]
Materials:
Potted plant: Green necklace
Cut flowers: Poppy, heather
Outer container: Wooden pail

Flower pot arrangements add festivity to wedding anniversary celebrations. The five varieties of cut flowers used here add elegance to the voluminous potted azalea laden with colorful flowers.

Materials:
Potted plant: Azalea
Cut flowers: Chrysanthemum, *Dendrobium phalaenopsis*, daffodil, *Asparagas myriocladus*, Thunberg's spirea
Outer container: White porcelain container

Create joyful exuberance when you arrange dramatic tropical flowers in this donkey-shaped rattan container.

Material:
Potted plant: Dracaena
Cut flowers: Strelitzia, jasmine (*Stephanotis floribunda*)
Outer container: Donkey-shaped rattan basket

Add a softly elegant ambiance to your bedroom by arranging eye-catching cut flowers with a densely growing potted romaria.

Materials:
Potted plant: Romaria
Cut flowers: Rose, oncidium orchid
Outer container: Steel container

This arrangement in a large rattan basket nicely complements any piece of furniture.

Materials:
Potted plant: Scotch broom
Cut flower: Anemone
Outer container: Rattan basket

Materials:
Potted plant: Ivy
Cut flowers: Aster, foxtail lily
  (loosestrife), star lily, marguerite
Outer container: Black ceramic
  pot

This flower pot arrangement is perfect for a traditional Japanese *tokonoma* alcove.
Materials:
Potted plant: Coralberry (*Ardisia crenata*) **Cut flowers:** Camellia, sasa bamboo, fringed iris leaves
Outer container: Ceramic pot

[At right:] You can add elegance to your home simply by placing a small arrangement in a quiet corner.
Materials:
Potted plant: Dimorphotheca **Cut flowers:** Bleached scotch broom **Outer container:** Rattan basket

This example shows that by adding a single pine branch to two Western plants—poinsettia and oncidium orchid—you can create a composition that is quite suitable for a Japanese-style room.

Materials:
Potted plant: Poinsettia
Cut flowers: Pine, oncidium orchid
Outer container: Rattan basket

Materials:
Potted plant: Begonia
Cut flowers: Gerbera, baby's breath
Outer container: Horn-shaped bamboo vase

Materials:
Potted plant: Palm
Cut flower: Gerbera
Outer container: Bamboo basket with a tall handle

Materials:
Potted plant: Croton
  (*Codiaeum variegatum*
  'Akebono')
Cut flowers: *Dendrobium pha-
  laenopsis*, statice caspia
Outer container: Rattan container

Materials:
Potted plant: Flamingo
  begonia (*Begonia ficicola*)
Cut flowers: Japanese astilbe, marguerite, glory lily (*Gloriosa*)
Outer container: White porcelain
  pot

Materials:
Potted plant: Repia
Cut flowers: Chinese ixora, lobelia
Outer container: Ceramic pot

Materials:
Potted plant: Anthurium
Cut flowers: Chinese bellflower, statice caspia
Outer container: Ceramic vase

Materials:
Potted plant: *Ficus benjamina*
 (Benjamin tree)
Cut flowers: Patrinia, bittersweet,
 gentian
Outer container: Rattan basket

Materials:
Potted plant: Croton
 (*Codiaeum variegatum* 'Akebono')
Cut flowers: Calla lily, godetia
Outer container: Glass container

Part 2

Basic Methods

I. Arranging Tall Potted Flowers

Potted plants with flowers at the tips of their erect stems have an uncomplicated beauty. To highlight this natural appeal, treat the top section of the flowers differently from the flowers' base. In the simplest form, Basic Form A, the potted flower by itself is made the high material, and cut flowers are added at the base to complete the composition. Because a tall outer container will make the flowers look taller, do not use one that is too high.

BASIC FORM A

This is the simplest form, using tall-stemmed potted flowers as the high material and cut flowers as the low material.

Example 1 (Basic Form A)

Materials:
Potted plant: Freesia
  (high material)
Cut flower: *Shiratama* camellia
  (low material)
Outer container: Decorative
  plastic pot

A freesia which has stems extending in various directions is the high material, and a single white camellia is inserted at the base as the low material. The freesia's beauty is emphasized here.

Arrangement:
1 Prepare a potted freesia.
2 Prepare an outer container which is deep enough to cover the pot.
3 Place a small square *kenzan* (spiked metal stand used to support stems) into the cone-shaped holder (*kenzutsu*) to secure the cut flower.

4 Insert the holder into the soil of the pot, tilting it slightly forward.

5–6 Arrange a camellia branch in the holder.

7 Add water to the holder.

BASIC FORM B

This form uses a potted plant as the high material and cut flowers as the middle and low materials. Strong, abundant materials are placed high and low, in contrast to the soft impression of the middle material, to create an interesting overall balance and harmony.

Example 1 (Basic Form B)
Materials:
Potted plant: Sasanqua camellia (high material)
Cut flowers: Freesia flowers and leaves (middle material); holly tree (low material)
Outer container: Ceramic pot

The potted sasanqua camellia in a high position and holly branches in a lower position lend strong impact. The gentle beauty of freesia flowers and leaves, the middle material, helps strike a balance between strength and softness.

Example 2 (Basic Form B)

This form includes high, middle and low materials using potted flowers for the middle material.

Materials:
Potted flower: *Shiratama* camellia (middle material)
Cut flowers: Freesia (high and middle materials); azalea leaves (low material)
Outer container: Bronze pot

Composition:
Because of its relatively sparse leaves and striking white flowers, the *shiratama* camellia should be the focus of the arrangement. To display its beauty to full effect, arrange only a few cut flowers, keeping the overall arrangement simple.

Arrangement:
1 Place the potted camellia in the outer container.

When using tall potted flowers with sparse leaves, employ an outer container which is deep enough to hide the base of the plant, so you can easily add cut flowers at the base.
2 To fill the space between the camellia and the outer container and to visually link the container with the floral materials, set the azalea branches at a low position without thinning out their small, dense leaves.
3 Arrange freesia flowers at a high position to create a sense of movement. To stabilize the arrangement, insert the freesia buds and leaves at the middle position.

Note:
To maintain a balance with the deep outer container, use only a few branches at the low position.

1

2

3

II. Arranging Upright, Long-stemmed Potted Flowers

Long-stemmed, upright flowers can come in many types, from thickly blooming flowers to plants with just one or two tiny blossoms. It is important to understand the features of each plant and to arrange the cut flowers in harmony with the colors and line of the potted plants. Low outer containers are suitable for this form.

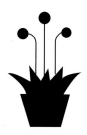

BASIC FORM A

This form uses the flower stems of a potted plant as the high material and its leaves as the low material, in combination with some cut flowers. If the potted plant has sparse leaves, select leafy cut flowers. For the opposite case, as in Example 4 below, add cut flowers with fewer leaves.

Example 1 (Basic Form A)
The leaves of the potted plant and the cut flowers are integrated at the base.

Materials:
Potted plant: *Paphiopedilum* orchid (flowers: upper position; leaves: lower position)
Cut flowers: *Senryo* (*Chloranthus glaber* Makino) (lower material)
Outer container: Ceramic pot

The interesting shape of the tall *paphiopedilum* flowers is displayed at the top of this arrangement. *Senryo* flowers are arranged to add volume and stability to the *paphiopedilum* leaves at the base. Because the *senryo* is combined with the *paphiopedilum* leaves at the base, this technique is called "low integration."

BASIC FORM B

There are high, middle and low materials in this arrangement, with the potted flower used in the high position.

This form uses the potted plant, with its overlapping flowers and leaves, as the middle material. Arranging cut flowers so that they extend horizontally makes for a striking composition.

Example 1 (Basic Form B)
An example of "middle flow" and "low integration"

Materials:
Potted plant: *Paphiopedilum* orchid (flowers: high position; leaves: low position)
Cut flowers: Thunberg's spirea (middle material); *senryo* (*Chloranthus glaber* Makino) (low material)
Outer container: Ceramic pot

The *senryo* and *paphiopedilum* leaves are integrated at the base (using the same *paphiopedilum* and the *senryo* branch at right as in Example 1), with a spirea branch arranged horizontally in the middle position for a "flowing" effect. In contrast to the serene impression of Example 1, this arrangement conveys an impression of movement and growth.

Example 2 (Basic Form B)
When the leaves of a potted plant remain green but the flowers wither and die, they can be replaced with some cut flowers.

Materials:
Potted plant: *Paphiopedilum* orchid leaves (low material)
Cut flowers: Carnation (high material)
Outer container: Red tin container

The leaves of orchid plants like the *paphiopedilum* remain green even after the flowers wither. To enjoy the potted plant during its flowerless season, the leaves are used as the low material with carnations added at a high position.

Note:
"*Fukugo* (integration or blending)" and "*Nagashi* (flowing)"
Fukugo in Japanese refers to the technique for integrating cut flowers harmoniously into a potted plant. In the lower part of Example 1, *senryo* (*Chloranthus* Sw.) leaves are placed so that they do not extend beyond the basic outline of the potted orchid and blend in with the plant's leaves. This style is called "low integration."

Nagashi is a common technique in *ikebana*, but it also applies to the flower pot ikebana arrangements described in this book. *Nagashi* literally means "flowing," and in Ikebana with Living Plants it refers to the technique in which a holder containing a branch is inserted in the soil at an angle, to look as if it were extending horizontally from the center. In Example 2, the spirea, the middle material, gives the illusion of "flowing"; therefore, this style is called "middle flow."

ARRANGING LONG-STEMMED POTTED FLOWERS

Example 3 (Basic Form B)
This form includes high, middle and low materials, with a potted plant used as the high material.

Materials:
Potted plant: Marguerite (high material)
Cut flowers: Anemone (middle material); statice (low material)
Outer container: Rattan basket

Composition:
This arrangement consists of high, middle and low materials, including a potted marguerite and cut flowers of anemone and statice.

Potted flowers such as marguerite, with tall, erect stems, are naturally used as the high material, and cut flowers are arranged at the middle and low positions to stabilize the composition. With the "flowing" technique, used at the middle position, you can change this form in some interesting ways.

Arrangement:
1 To complement the marguerite flowers, which some say are the quintessential Japanese flower, use an open, Oriental rattan basket for the outer container.
2 Arrange anemone at the middle position for a splash of color. But take care not to use too many anemone, because these strong flowers might steal the focus from the main material, the marguerite flowers.
3 Arrange statice near the base of the arrangement. In order to visually integrate the low and middle materials, vary the heights of the statice.

Note:
When arranging cut flowers with potted flowers, use a limited number of cut flowers, to retain the focus on the potted plant.

3

Example 4 (Basic Form B)

This form includes high, middle and low materials with a horizontal extension.

Materials:

Potted plant: Cyclamen (flowers: high material; leaves: low material)

Cut flowers: Nandina leaves (middle material); nandina berries (low material)

Outer container: Plastic basket

This potted cyclamen has few flowers, lending a barren look to the plant. To add vitality, a cluster of red nandina berries are added, with branches of nandina leaves extending horizontally from the center.

Example 5 (Basic Form B)

This form includes high, middle and low materials, emphasizing mass.

Materials:

Potted plant: Cyclamen (flowers: upper position; leaves: lower position)

Cut flowers: Dwarf asparagus fern leaves (*Asparagus plumosus*) (middle material)

Outer container: Ceramic pot (made by Ryoei Nishida)

The dainty, airy asparagus leaves are arranged around the potted cyclamen, with its mass of tall, erect flowers and lower leafy stems. The composition gives a solid impression overall.

Example 6 (Basic Form B)
This form includes high and low materials that integrate varied linear and plane characteristics.

Materials:
Potted plant: Spathe flower (*Spathiphyllum*) (flowers: high material; leaves: low material)
Cut flowers: Gerbera (low material); narcissus leaves (low material)
Outer container: Ceramic pot

In stark contrast to the wide, drooping leaves, one spathe flower blossom stands tall and erect. This distinctive feature is highlighted by having the flower stand alone as the high material, and inserting gerbera flowers at a low position

so as not to detract from the beauty of the broad, rich green leaves. The linear narcissus leaves are added for contrast with the flat, wide-surfaced spathe flower leaves. This is an example of the technique of "low integration."

Example 7 (Basic Form B)
This form includes high and low materials using a pot of cyclamen and a branch of *shiratama* camellia.

Materials:
Potted plant: Cyclamen (high material)
Cut flower: *Shiratama* camellia (low material)
Outer container: Tin container (place a platform inside to raise the level of the pot)

To highlight the unique lines and dense leaves of the cyclamen, a single white camellia is inserted in the foreground as a striking accent. A single flower can change the overall impression of the potted cyclamen immensely.

ARRANGING LONG-STEMMED POTTED FLOWERS

Example 8 (Basic Form B)
Materials:
Potted plant: Ageratum
Cut flowers: Patrinia, chestnut
  branch
Outer container: Bamboo basket

With a simple bamboo basket and a chestnut branch, you can create an arrangement with an autumn feeling.

Arrangement:
1 Place the potted ageratum in the bamboo basket. Use the flowers as the middle material.
2 Insert a chestnut branch at the base extending horizontally forward and to the left.
3 Arrange the yellow patrinia stems in both low and high positions among the ageratum leaves and flowers for an interesting color contrast. Add a few stems at the base to highlight the natural line of the chestnut.

3

III. ARRANGING DENSELY BLOOMING POTTED FLOWERS

Some densely blooming plants have a relatively low weight center, while others are massed at a higher position. In both cases the flowers and leaves combine to form a dense mass. For this type of potted flower, you should add delicate soft cut flowers as focal or linear complements. Using a variety of outer containers creates a wide range of interesting effects: Deep containers make a plant look larger and larger ones reduce the impact of the arrangement, while a bamboo basket creates quite a different atmosphere.

BASIC FORM A

This is the simplest form, using a voluminous potted flower as the low material and cut flowers in a high position. To balance the massed flowers at the base, you should arrange linear cut flowers at a high position for a most attractive composition.

Example 1 (Basic Form A)
This form includes high and low materials, highlighting the contrast between linear and massed materials.

Materials:
Potted flower: Riegers begonia (low material)
Cut flowers: Thunberg's spirea (high material)
Outer container: Plastic pot

Using a potted begonia as the low material and spirea as the high material emphasizes the interesting contrast between mass and line. This is one of the simplest examples of this form.

Example 2 (Basic Form A)
This form includes high and low materials. With its use of Western materials, it suggests a European-style arrangement.

Materials:
Potted flower: Primrose julian
   (low material)
Cut flower: Baby's breath (high
   material)
Outer container: White porcelain
   vase

Using a tall, white porcelain vase for the outer container, arrange a small mass of potted primrose at a low position. High above it arrange baby's breath, which spreads its flowers in all directions, to create an elegant composition. Insert the cut flower holder as close as possible to the center of the pot.

Example 3 (Basic Form A)
This form includes Japanese and Western materials in the high and low positions.

Materials:
Potted flower: Primrose julian
   (low material)
Cut flowers: *Shiratama* camellia
   (high material)
Outer container: Ceramic pot
   (made by Ryoei Nishida)

This example uses the primrose as in Example 2 above, but the use of a camellia, which conveys a Japanese feeling, nicely stabilizes the arrangement. Insert a cut flower holder as close as possible to the center of the pot.

1

4

3

2

ARRANGING DENSELY BLOOMING POTTED FLOWERS

Example 4 (Basic Form A)
Materials:
Potted plant: *Cineraria multipolar*
Cut flowers: Reeves spirea, snap-
  dragon, freesia
Outer container: Panama hat

In this arrangement, snapdragon and freesia are integrated into the potted cineraria at the high and middle positions. By arranging the spirea branches to extend dramatically from a high position, a contrast between solidity and dynamism is created in this composition.

Because spirea branches have elegant curving lines, they are used at a high position, extending to both right and left. By integrating them into the cineraria at high and middle positions, you emphasize the contrast between mass and line.

Arrangement
1 Before placing the potted cineraria into the outer container, choose the most attractive face to set in front of the plant. Remove

5

any withered flowers or damaged
leaves.

2–3 Arrange the spirea branches
at the center to extend far to the
right and left, creating a contrast
between the mass and the curving
lines.

4–5 Add the snapdragon at the
center at a low position to consolidate the base of the arrangement
and to visually unify the spirea and
cineraria. Insert the freesia at a low
position as a color accent.

BASIC FORM B

This form uses a densely blooming potted flower as the high material and cut flowers as the low material. It is important to arrange the cut flowers as focal points or for linear contrast, and to vary the amount of color of the materials used in the arrangement.

Example 1 (Basic Form B)
Materials:
Potted flower: Riegers begonia (flowers: high material; leaves: low material)
Cut flowers: Dwarf asparagus fern (*Asparagus plumosus*) leaves (low material); daffodil (low material)
Outer container: Three-legged copper container

This example uses begonia flowers as the high material, and a mass of linear asparagus leaves and begonia leaves near the base. Daffodils are added as focal points at a low position. By varying the amount of white, green and yellow in the arrangement, an interesting dynamism is achieved.

Example 2 (Basic Form B)

This form includes high, middle and low materials with linear, mass and wide-surfaced aspects.

Materials:

Potted flower: Azalea (middle material)

Cut flowers: Thunberg's spiraea leaves tinged in red (high material); dieffenbachia (low material)

Outer container: Ceramic pot

With the linear spirea branches at a high position, a mass of potted azalea arranged at the middle position and the wide-surfaced dieffenbachia leaves set low at the left, the three basic characters of plant materials are ingeniously represented in this arrangement.

Example 3 (Basic Form B)

This form includes high, middle and low materials, for a strongly three-dimensional arrangement.

Materials:

Potted flower: Cineraria (low material)

Cut flowers: Japanese miscanthus (Eulalia)(high material); narcissus (low material)

Outer container: Ceramic pot

In this example, the high Japanese miscanthus stems wave gracefully above the daffodils at the middle position and the cineraria at the base, forming a unique three-dimensional composition.

IV. ARRANGING LOW, COMPACT-BODIED POTTED FLOWER

For potted plants which have flowers and leaves growing at a low position, such as miniature begonias, primula, saintpaulia and marigold, there are three basic ways of arranging cut flowers, as explained below.

BASIC FORM A

This form uses cut flowers as the high material and a potted plant as the low material.

Example 1 (Basic Form A)
Materials:
Potted plant: Riegers begonia
Cut flowers: Iris
Outer container: Basket

In this arrangement, there is much empty space between the tall cut flowers and the low-growing potted plant. The composition may appear unbalanced, but by arranging the cut flowers at a high position, we further emphasize the contrasting characteristics of the high and low materials, and the whole arrangement gains greater vitality.

BASIC FORM B

This form uses cut flowers as high and middle materials and a potted plant as a low material.

Example 1 (Basic Form B)
Materials:
Potted plant: Riegers begonia
Cut flowers: Elegant lily, small chrysanthemum
Outer container: Basket

This is a very solid, stable composition. However, if the high, middle and low sections of the arrangement have the same volume, the composition will be tedious and lacking in rhythmical movement. To avoid this, arrange the middle material relatively low to create a sense of flow.

BASIC FORM C

This form uses some cut flowers as the high material and other cut flowers and a potted plant as the low material.

Example 1 (Basic Form C)
Materials:
Potted plant: Riegers begonia
Cut flowers: Carnation, single stock
Outer container: Basket

The height proportions of the arrangement are the same as in Form A, but the low section is more abundant. Be careful not to add too many cut flowers in a low position to avoid overwhelming the flowers of the potted plant. Add just a modest amount for a color accent.

1

2

ARRANGING LOW, COMPACT-BODIED POTTED FLOWERS

Example 2 (Basic Form C)
Materials:
Potted plant: Christmas cactus
Cut flowers: Nandina berries
Outer container: Bamboo basket with a handle

Although potted plants such as Christmas cactus and crab's claw cactus, which have flowers bloom-

ing at the end of each pendulous leaf, are usually categorized separately, in this book they are treated as "low compact-bodied potted flowers." They are best arranged at a low position. Because their flowers and stems extend downward, when arranging cut flowers at a high position, try to make the arrangement attractively asymmetric by using only a few cut flowers. Alternatively, you can add a sense of stability by having the branches flow downward.

Arrangement:
1 Since Christmas cactus grows both outward and downward, set the pot atop a platform in a deep container so it will sit at a high level. This makes it much easier to arrange the plant.
2 To fill the space between the handle of the basket and the cactus, and to add a color accent, arrange red nandina berries at a high position.
3 Arrange the nandina branches so they extend far out to the right and

3

left, adding volume to the arrangement. Be careful not to hide the cactus flowers behind the nandina leaves.

Key Point
When arranging cut branches in a horizontal movement on both sides and to add asymmetric interest, set the center of the composition slightly to one side by using a longer branch on one side.

V. ARRANGING TALL, LEAFY POTTED PLANTS

Some of the many varieties of tall, leafy potted plants have many large, well-spaced leaves which grow from a single stem (like the dracaena), while others feature densely growing leaves and stems. Arrange these tall potted plants to emphasize their most outstanding features: For tall, leafy plants for instance, treat the top of the plant differently than the lower portion in an arrangement. When you use a deep outer container, try to conceal as much of the base of the plant as possible for better visual balance. If you prefer a shallow container, choose one that is large, with a wide mouth.

BASIC FORM A

This form leaves the natural line of the leafy potted plant at the top. Cut flowers are arranged near the base to complete the arrangement.

Example 1 (Basic Form A)
Materials:
Potted plant: Dracaena corderine 'crystal' (high material)
Cut flowers: Rape flower (low material)
Outer container: Wide plastic bowl

In this simple form, the volume of the top material varies from that of the low material. In this example, the slender features of the dracaena are displayed at the top, and two branches of rape flower are arranged at the base.

Arrangement:
1 Prepare a potted plant.
2 Prepare an outer container suitable for the plant.
3 Place the plant inside the outer container.
4 Place a *kenzan* inside the cone-shaped holder.
5 Insert the holder into the soil of the pot.

6 Insert cut flowers into the holder.
7 Pour water into the holder.

3

4

5

6

7

Front view

Side view

57

BASIC FORM B

This form uses the upper portion of a potted plant as the high material and two different kinds of cut flowers arranged in the middle and low positions.

Example 1 (Basic Form B)
In this example, heather has been added at the middle position of the arrangement.

Materials:
Potted plant: Dracaena corderine 'crystal' (high material)
Cut flowers: Heather (middle material); rape flower (low material)
Outer container: Plastic bowl

This arrangement consists of high, middle and low materials, with heather added at a middle position. The heather is arranged to extend sideways, adding a flowing movement to the whole composition.

Example 2 (Basic Form B)

This form includes high, middle and low materials, with an unusually shaped basket used as the outer container.

Materials:

Potted plant: Dracaena corderine 'crystal' (high material)

Cut flowers: Bouvardia (middle material); lily (middle and low material)

Outer container: Basket

The shape of this particular basket, with its wide handle, influences the arrangement of low and middle materials. The dracaena leaves alone are at the top, but they are joined at the middle position by the bouvardia and the lilies, which are integrated with them ("middle integration").

Example 3 (Basic Form B)

This is an example of "overall integration" with a deep outer container.

Materials:

Potted plant: Dracaena corderine 'crystal'

Cut flowers: Freesia, rose, *Dendrobium phalaenopsis* orchid

Outer container: Deep rattan basket (place a platform inside the basket to raise the level of the potted plant)

The freesia and roses are arranged so that they can be integrated effectively with the potted dracaena leaves. Although the orchid stems spill out from the mouth of the basket, creating a sense of downward movement, they don't spoil the overall line of the dracaena, so this arrangement can be considered an example of "overall integration." The beauty of this arrangement lies in its colorful combination of green, yellow, red and pink.

1

2

ARRANGING TALL LEAFY POTTED PLANTS

Example 4 (Basic Form B)
Materials:
Potted plant: Ponytail (*Beaucarnea recurvata*)
Cut flowers: Glory lily (*Gloriosa*), baby's breath
Outer container: Metal pot

The tall potted ponytail is ideal for the high material. You should avoid using delicate or wispy cut flowers as the low material, since you will have little contrast between the upper and the lower section; instead, use rather voluminous flowers.

Arrangement:
1 Use a large metal pot as the outer container to balance with the tall ponytail.
2 Arrange glory lily at a low position to fill the space near the base and to link the ponytail with the outer container.
3 Arrange baby's breath at the middle position to soften the effect at the center of the arrangement.

3

VI. Arranging Densely Growing Leafy Potted Plants

Some leafy, densely growing potted plants have large leaves and others have smaller leaves, but all feature leaves overlapping to form a mass of foliage. Arranging dense leafy potted plants near the mouth of the outer container and cut flowers at the high and middle positions will yield an overall sense of mass and a stable balance of proportions. Potted leafy plants whose stems lack leaves at their base can be arranged at a high position, or they can be arranged low, where their lower stems can be hidden by the outer container. Use of a fairly shallow outer container makes it easier to create an attractive composition.

BASIC FORM A

This simple composition features dense foliage arranged at the mouth of the container and cut flowers at a high position.

Example 1 (Basic Form A)
Materials:
Potted plant: Maidenhair fern (*Adiantum*) (low material)
Cut flowers: *Senryo* (*Chloranthus glaber* Makino) (high material)
Outer container: Rattan basket with a tall handle

The potted maidenhair fern is placed into the basket so as to conceal its lower stems. The maidenhair fern is arranged near the mouth and the senryo at a high position.

BASIC FORM B

For this form, arrange a leafy potted plant at a high position and cut flowers near the base.

Example 1 (Basic Form B)
Materials:
Potted plant: The same maiden hair fern (*Adiantum*) as in Basic Form A and C examples (middle material)
Cut flowers: Lily (low material)
Outer container: Ceramic pot

Because leaves are sparse on the lower stems of the potted maidenhair fern, arrange lilies at the base to fill the space and to add stability at the bottom of the composition.

BASIC FORM C

In this composition, a densely growing leafy potted plant is arranged at a middle position and

some cut flowers are set near the base to hide the lower part of the stems. Different types of cut flowers are arranged at a high position to extend above the leaves. In order to harmonize with the mass in the middle, arrange cut flowers as focal points or linear complements at both the high and low positions.

Example 1 (Basic Form C)
Materials:
Potted plants: The same maidenhair fern (*Adiantum*) as in Basic Form A and B examples (middle material)
Cut flowers: Bouvardia (high material); lily (low material)
Outer container: The same flower container as in the Basic Form B example

Bouvardia is added to the Basic Form B arrangement at a high position. To balance the solid mass at the middle, this composition features cut flowers as linear complements at the top and as focal points at the base.

Example 2 (Basic Form B)

Materials:

Potted plant: Maidenhair fern
(*Adiantum*)

Cut flowers: Gerbera (high material), miniature rose (middle material), aster pansy (high material)

Outer container: Wooden pot

This dense and leafy potted maidenhair fern occupies the high, middle and low positions, so when you add cut flowers, try to integrate them with the fern leaves at each position to create a balanced composition. Because the maidenhair fern looks soft and delicate, add several cut flowers to add weight to the arrangement. To make the arrangement look more stable, add to the middle and low positions.

Arrangement:

1 For a voluminous plant with a large, lush form like the maidenhair fern, a low outer container is the most suitable. A wooden pot is used here. Place the potted maidenhair fern in the center of the outer container.

2 For contrast with the maidenhair fern's green leaves, arrange the brightly colored gerbera prominently at a high position.

3–4 Arrange the miniature roses at the left of the middle section. Insert the aster pansies at a high position to integrate with the maidenhair fern leaves and provide a color accent.

1

2

3

4

ARRANGING DENSELY GROWING LEAFY POTTED PLANTS

In these examples of "overall integration," the cut flowers blend with the green leaves of the potted plant.

Example 3 (Basic Form B)
Materials:
Potted plant: Dieffenbachia
Cut flowers : Glory lily (*Gloriosa*), baby's breath
Outer container: Ceramic pot

Example 4 (Basic Form B)
Materials:
Potted plant: Maidenhair fern (*Adiantum*)
Cut flowers: Carnation
Outer container: Ceramic container (made by Ryoei Nishida)

These examples show "overall integration," with cut flowers combined with the green leaves. If the cut flower holder is placed close to the center of the pot, it will be easier to unify the cut flowers with the green leaves.

Example 5 (Basic Form B)
This form includes high, middle and low materials with linear and wide-surfaced elements.

Materials:
Potted plant: *Dracaena fragrans* 'massangeana' (low material)
Cut flowers: Paulownia berries (high material); prairie gentian (middle material)
Outer container: Ceramic compote

The potted dracaena is set deep within the outer container to emphasize its wide-surfaced leaves near the mouth of the container, and the paulownia berries are

treated as focal points at the top. The prairie gentian are inserted at a middle position for a color accent.

Example 6 (Basic Form B)
This form includes high and low materials, with cut flowers integrated in the leafy mass at the base.

Materials:
Potted plant: African evergreen (*Syngonium podophyllum*) (low material)
Cut flowers: Bristle grass (high material); narcissus (low material)
Outer container: Copper pot

The large, overlapping leaves of the potted *Syngonium podophyllum* are integrated with the delicate narcissus at the base of the arrangement. The linear, tall-stemmed bristle grass fills out the top of the form.

VII. ARRANGING POTTED PLANTS WITH LOW, COMPACT LEAVES

Because this type of plant has leaves growing very low, it cannot be arranged at a high position. The potted plant, therefore, is arranged near the mouth of the container, with cut flowers at the high or middle positions. Densely growing potted plants can also be used in this type of arrangement by placing them deep within the outer container.

BASIC FORM A

This is the most conventional form, with the potted plant used as the low material and cut flowers arranged at a high position.

Example 1 (Basic Form A)
Materials:
Potted plant: Basket plant (*Aeschynanthus*) (low material)
Cut flowers: Shiratama camellia (high material)
Outer container: Plastic flower pot

To simplify this arrangement as much as possible, only a single camellia branch is used at a high position. By retaining a large space between the high and low materials, the beauty of both materials is emphasized, and the space itself becomes an interesting feature of the arrangement.

BASIC FORM B

This form uses a potted plant as the low material and cut flowers at the high and middle positions. As the high and middle materials are tall and extend horizontally, they should be balanced by use of a wide outer container.

Example 1 (Basic Form B)
Materials:
Potted plant: The same basket plant (*Aeschynanthus*) as in the Basic Form A example (low material)
Cut flowers: Asparagus fern (*Asparagus plumosus*) (high material); rose (middle material)
Outer container: Bamboo basket

Using a wide outer container gives the base of the arrangement a more solid appearance, while making the arrangement as a whole look larger. The showy roses are tightly bunched together in the middle, to maximize the gentle sideways movement of the asparagus fern up above. Insert the cut flower holder near the center of the pot.

1

2

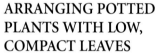
3

ARRANGING POTTED PLANTS WITH LOW, COMPACT LEAVES

Several of the plants featured in previous arrangements, including potted plants with dangling stems, upright, long-stemmed potted plants, and densely blooming potted flowers, can be treated the same as potted plants with low-growing, compact leaves.

Example 2 (Basic Form B)
This form includes high, middle and low materials, with a potted plant as the low and middle materials.

Materials:
Potted plant: One red, one white ornamental cabbage (low and middle materials)
Cut flowers: Thunberg's spirea (high and middle materials); marguerite (high material); gerbera (middle material)
Outer container: Two-level ceramic basin

Composition:
With the two heavy, voluminous ornamental cabbage plants set low

in the container at different levels, you can create a sense of movement using cut flowers. To balance the dense form of the cabbage, select cut flowers with linear characteristics. The spirea and marguerite used in this arrangement are both linear; the former has elegant lines, while the latter is more delicate. In order to fully bring out their qualities, try to arrange the spirea in a large space, to create dynamic movement. Arrange the marguerite more compactly, to subtly accent the arrangement.

Arrangement:
1 Set the two different colored ornamental cabbage plants in the container as the middle and low materials. Because the lower portion consists of only cabbage, try to select a nicely colored, highly expressive plant. The cabbage arranged above it should be coarser in appearance, as it will be integrated with the cut flowers.
2 Insert the two gerbera low at a middle position at the center of the arrangement, so that they can be integrated with the cabbage, while at the same time visually linking the two cabbage plants.

Arrange their flower faces so they face in different directions.
3 Add the spirea at the high and middle positions. Use a multistemmed branch of spirea for the high material, arranging it to extend almost horizontally. Insert another spirea branch as a middle material, and have it extend to the forward right to add depth to the

70

4

arrangement.
4 Add several marguerite flowers
at the left at a high position to lend
softness and stability to the entire
composition.

VIII. ARRANGING POTTED PLANTS WITH DANGLING STEMS

Many plants with dangling stems tend to have vines or stems extending from the tips of their leaves. During the vineless season, treat them as you do densely growing leafy plants. In order to emphasize the downward movement of the stems, they should be arranged at a low position. When the stems are very short, the cut flowers arranged at the top should be kept fairly low. The appeal of this type of plant lies in the movement of the dangling leaves. This can be best highlighted by using a deep outer container. To create a unified composition, insert a cut flower holder near the center of the pot.

Example 2

BASIC FORM A

This form includes high and low materials, with a potted plant arranged at a low position.

In this form, the beauty of the dangling leaves should be emphasized at the base of the arrangement and the cut flowers above should be kept fairly low.

Example 1 (Basic Form A)
Materials:
Potted plant: Spiderwort
   (*Tradescantia*) (low material)
Cut flowers: Bouvardia
   (high material)
Outer container: Deep woven
   rattan container (place a tall platform within it to elevate the potted plant.)

The bouvardia at the top is arranged rather low. Just a few flowers emerging from the leaves can create sufficient upper space.

Example 2 (Basic Form A)
Materials:
Potted plant: The same spiderwort as in the Basic Form A example (low material)
Cut flowers: Maple leaves (high material); anthurium (high material); mountain ash berries (high material)
Outer container: Ceramic container

Because the stems of the potted spiderwort are not yet fully grown, the shape is similar to that of densely growing leafy plants. The anthurium is arranged low in the upper position, with the maple branch creating a linear flow to the left.
(See photograph on opposite page, right)

BASIC FORM B

Cut flowers are integrated with the leaves of the potted plant.

Example 1 (Basic Form B)
Materials:
Potted plant: The same spiderwort as in Examples 1 and 2
Cut flowers: Rose
Outer container: The same rattan container as in Example 1

1–3 The roses are arranged especially low so that they will combine with the leaves to create an elegant color accent.

Example 2 (Basic Form B)
This is an example of "overall integration," emphasizing the natural flow of the stems.

Materials:
Potted plant: African evergreen (*Syngonium podophyllum*)
Cut flowers: Chrysanthemum
Outer container: Rattan basket

To use the dynamic, fast-growing branches to best effect, the cut flowers are inserted to form a solid mass. The chrysanthemum are bunched and integrated with the green leaves in two places.

Example 3 (Basic Form B)
This is an example of "overall integration" using a deep outer container.

Materials:
Potted plant: *Senryo* (*Chloranthus glaber* Makino)
Cut flowers: Mountain ash berries, *Dendrobium phalaenopsis*
Outer container: Rattan container

The vitality of the potted *senryo*, with its stems growing in all directions, is brought out by using a deep outer container. Branches of red mountain ash berries and pink orchids are integrated with the green leaves to create an arrangement of striking beauty.

Example 4 (Basic Form B)
This form includes high, middle and low materials with a potted plant arranged at the middle and low positions.

Materials:
Potted plant: Ribbon plant (*Chlorophrum comosum*) (middle and low material)
Cut flowers: Freesia (high material); tinted mountain ash (middle material); tinted Thunberg's spirea (middle material)
Outer container: Deep rattan container

The ribbon plant, with its dense leaves, is arranged at the middle of the arrangement, and the branches of red mountain ash and spirea leaves are integrated into it. With the ribbon plant's hanging leaf clusters, which resemble folded paper cranes, far below, two focal points are achieved in the arrangement. At the top, the freesia stems create vertical movement. Though the freesia is arranged at a high position, it maintains a suitable balance, thanks to its deliicate lines.

ARRANGING POTTED PLANTS WITH DANGLING STEMS

BASIC FORM C

This form includes high and low materials, with cut flowers integrated with the leaves of the potted plant at the base.

Example 1 (Basic Form C)
Materials:
Potted plant: Japanese ivy (low material)
Cut flowers: Chinese miscanthus (high material); gentian (high and low materials)
Outer container: Ceramic pot

Tassels of Chinese miscanthus are arranged at a high position to form the upper part of the composition, and a potted red-tinted Japanese ivy and gentian flowers are integrated at the base. The swordlike Chinese miscanthus leaves are used at both the high and low positions to create "*nagashi*" (flowing movement). In the high position, they "flow" to both the right and the left, thus broadening the scale of the arrangement. Below, they are integrated with the dangling leaves of the potted plant to cause subtle changes in the composition.

Arrangement:
1 Arrange tassels of Chinese miscanthus, varying their height and the directions they face, for the upper part of the composition. Arrange one of the linear Chinese miscanthus leaves at a high position and the others at a low position.
2 Add two more Chinese miscanthus tassels at the top to create an autumn atmosphere. Arrange some more Chinese miscanthus leaves at a high position for a flow-

3

ing effect, adding dynamic movement to the arrangement.

3 Add a few gentian stems at the center near the base to form a central focus and to tighten up the arrangement as a whole.

Note:
When using Chinese miscanthus for a flowing effect, separate the tassels from the leaves beforehand.

Part 3

Arrangements in Season

In Japan our flower arranging traditions are closely linked to the seasons.
An example is the still commonly practiced custom of
creating a formal New Year's arrangement of pine,
bamboo and other plants.
By incorporating the virtues of such traditions into
our modern potted plant arrangements,
we can create a fresh, attractive approach to arranging that fits perfectly
with our contemporary living spaces.

Spring and Summer

Spring is a time of cheer, and you can herald the arrival of this glorious season by incorporating a variety of colorful flowers in your arrangements. A great number of potted flowers and leafy plants will become available at florists' shops when the fresh leaves on the trees begin to bud. Follow this basic principle in arranging Ikebana with Living Plants: If a potted plant has plenty of flowers, arrange leafy plants as the complementary cut materials; if the potted plant is leafy, use flowering plants as the cut materials. The great variety of floral materials on the market allows us to experiment with all kinds of variations of the basic forms. For instance, if a potted plant has large, voluminous flowers, use differently colored cut flowers with a dainty feel to convey the lightness of the season. The room temperature starts to rise gradually around this time, so always remember to keep the plants fresh by adding water to the cut flower holders every morning and evening.

In Japan, the arrival of the oppressive rainy season in mid-June makes for a heavier atmosphere. You can dispel the gloom by making fresh, brightly colored arrangements. Try to choose plants that will make the viewer feel cooler and refreshed, rather than massive potted plants or densely growing leafy plants, and add only a small number of cut flowers to an arrangement. One successful approach to arranging in this season is to combine a flowery potted plant with a variety of colorful cut flowers, for a radiant impact. You can highlight this bright effect by using warm-toned flowers for the main body of the arrangement and adding an accent of a few cool-toned blossoms. On sunny days, don't forget to place potted plants, which need abundant sunshine, in the sun.

Summer flowers that bloom in the glittering sunshine tend to be of brighter hues, and they often have a lively appeal. These same flowers, when set in an arrangement, will continue to project strength, but they often make the viewer feel hot and heavy. To create arrangements that are strong but cool in appearance, try using fewer flowers than usual, incorporating plants found by the waterside, or using cool-toned flowers for the main body of the arrangement. Glass vases or baskets made of bamboo or rattan are good choices for the outer containers. Remember to change the water in the flower holder frequently. If you remove the flowers from the holder and place them in cold water overnight, they will last longer.

Autumn and Winter

When the summer flowers start to droop and a cooling autumn breeze begins to blow, the delicately lovely fall flowers begin blooming. Autumn flowers, in general, exhibit a poised, dewy grace, while most autumn grasses, such as Chinese miscanthus and patrinia, have a natural, uncomplicated appeal. One of the most important points to remember when arranging during this season is to highlight the rich beauty of the autumn materials.

As the season progresses, we can create a warm autumn atmosphere inside our homes by using potted plants and cut materials which convey a rich autumnal feeling. For cut materials, we can select from the many kinds of autumn grasses as well as branches which bear fruit, berries or nuts, or branches laden with tinted leaves. Good examples of such autumn materials include bittersweet and greenbrier berries, chestnuts and persimmon branches.

In late autumn, when the leaves begin to fall, the florists' shops start to fill with various kinds of winter flowers. We can create uniquely appealing arrangements at this time by setting them in interesting outer containers.

Towards the end of the year, an abundant mix of flowers and potted plants begin to bloom. A variety of leafy green plants and flowers like cyclamen, poinsettia and various kinds of orchids, including cattleya, oncidium, cymbidium and dendrobium, all compete for our attention. It can be very pleasant to decorate your rooms with flowers and enjoy the serene ambiance they can create. In fact, this just may be the best time to arrange flowers, because of the rich variety of floral materials from which to choose, and because you need not take as much care as in other seasons in replenishing the water. However, when using a room heater, make sure to change the water frequently.

At New Year's, Japanese create arrangements combining plants that are considered auspicious or traditional favorites, including pine, bamboo, wintergreen or nandina. To lend richer color to the arrangement, we often include such colorful cut flowers as orchids, roses and freesia. When carefully arranged in an impressive outer container, the composition will convey a powerful yet graceful beauty.

Spring 1

Materials:
Potted plant: Coralberry
 (*Ardisia crenata*)
Cut flowers: Pine, *Dendrobium
 phalaenopsis* orchids
Outer container: Bamboo vase

This is a New Year's arrangement
which uses a special bamboo container called a *shishiko* (lion's
mouth) as the outer container.

Arrangement:
1 Select the smallest size potted
coralberry available, and carefully
wash its roots. Then cover the
roots with peat moss and place the
plant in the bamboo container.

2 Prepare small pine branches
with thick needles. Insert them at a
forward slant so they extend horizontally, to give depth to the composition. Arrange a stem of
orchids to cover the mouth of the
container.

Spring 2

Materials:
Potted plant: Christmas cactus
Cut flowers: Willow, nandina,
  marigold, bamboo
Outer container: Bamboo basket
  with a handle

The Christmas cactus, with its
expressive sideways and downward movement, becomes the
focus of this arrangement.
Nandina and marigold are integrated at a low position as color
accents.

Arrangement:
1 Place the potted Christmas cactus in the bamboo basket and
arrange its stems and flowers so as
to cover the mouth of the container.
2 To balance the abundant Christmas cactus, arrange the bamboo at
a high position to convey a feeling
of lightness. Form a long willow
branch into a loop, with its tip
touching the floor. Arrange the
marigold and nandina at a low
position.

Spring 3

Materials:
Potted plant: Freesia
Cut flowers: Pine, Chinese toon
Outer container: Bamboo basket

This arrangement uses freesia as the high material, taking advantage of its upright line, and a branch of Chinese toon rich with red berries as the middle material. A small pine branch at the base adds stability to the arrangement.

Arrangement:
1 Arrange the freesia in a large bamboo basket with a handle. To hide some of the empty space inside the basket, prop the lid up against the front of the basket, covering the right half.
2 Arrange the Chinese toon at the middle position slightly to the left of center, to highlight the flow of the freesia leaves. Place the pine branch at a low forward position to complete the composition.

Spring 4

Materials:
Potted plant: *Begonia semperflorens*
Cut flowers: Gerbera, camellia,
  senryo (*Chloranthus glaber*
  Makino)
Outer container: Bamboo container

This arrangement uses a potted begonia which is just starting to bloom in early spring as the middle material and, by simply adding a branch of *senryo* at a higher position, adds a sense of movement. Two large gerbera flowers are inserted at a low middle position to stabilize the composition. The camellias are arranged to flow forward and to the left at the mouth of the container to add unity to the arrangement's diverse elements.

Arrangement:
1 When you combine Western and Japanese flowers in an arrangement, choose materials with completely different characters. Be sure to appropriately combine flower buds and blossoms.
2 Since the potted flowers are blooming all over the plant, add cut flowers for accent and focus. Arrange the high material lightly, for a sense of movement.

Insert the short camellia branches through the side openings in the bamboo basket.

85

Spring 5

Materials:
Potted plant: Cyclamen
Cut flowers: Dwarf asparagus fern
   (*Asparagus plumosus*), stock,
   narcissus
Outer container: Copper pot

This is a very colorful arrangement, with the red potted cyclamen and yellow narcissus flowers
waving above a cluster of stock
flowers, all of which are enveloped
in a dynamic green cloud of
asparagus fern leaves.

Arrangement:
1 Place the potted cyclamen in the
container.

2 Add the asparagus fern all
around the red cyclamen flowers.
To avoid creating a static, bulky
impression and add a sense of
movement, vary the proportions
and lengths of the material on the
right and left.

   Add the yellow narcissus and
the stock for additional color and
a tighter composition.

Spring 6

Materials:
Potted plant: Smilax asparagus
Cut flowers: Baby's breath,
  epidendrum orchid
Outer container: Ceramic
  container

This arrangement consists mainly
of the green potted smilax asparagus, but baby's breath and red epidendrum flowers have been added
at a high position as color accents.

Arrangement:
1 To enable the uniquely expressive smilax asparagus to be best
appreciated, add only a few cut
flowers.

2 Arrange the baby's breath to fill
the space at the upper right of the
arrangement; add the red epidendrum to complete the composition.

Spring 7

Materials:
Potted plants: Tamarisk tree
(*Munuka*)
Cut flowers: Thunberg's spirea,
narcissus
Outer container: Plastic flower pot

Arrangement:
1 Use the potted Tamarisk tree as
the middle material for a sense of
stability. Arrange the multi-
branched spirea to add a sense of
movement throughout the composition. These "flowing" branches should extend slightly forward.
2 Because the potted tamarisk has
densely growing branches, it is
arranged with the spirea, whose

sense of movement adds lightness
to the arrangement.
Arrange the narcissus so that
each flower faces in a slightly different direction.

Spring 8

Materials:
Potted plant: Maranta
Cut flower: Iceland poppy
Outer container: Ceramic pot

Arrangement:
1 The focus of this arrangement is the potted maranta, with its beautifully patterned leaves. Iceland poppies add charm to the arrangement.

2 Integrate a cluster of open Iceland poppy flowers among the lower maranta leaves.

Add a half-open poppy flower and flower buds at a high position. Their rhythmic flow will nicely counterbalance the bottom half of the composition.

Spring 9

Materials:
Potted plants: Ivy
Cut flowers: Sweet pea, narcissus
Outer container: Rattan basket

The potted ivy has drooping branches, from which extend beautiful dark green leaves. When adding cut flowers, set them at a low position to form a focal point, so you can achieve a good overall balance. A deep container is suitable for this arrangement.

Arrangement:
1 Place the potted ivy in a deep rattan basket and arrange it so that the ivy leaves cover and flow out over the basket's rim.
2 Insert a small bunch of sweet pea for a color accent.

Add some more sweet pea and narcissus, varying their heights.

Spring 10

Materials:
Potted plant: Scotch broom
Cut flowers: Iris, anemone
Outer container: Plastic flower pot

Scotch broom features bright green leaves with lovely yellow butterfly-like flowers extending in all directions. Iris and anemone flowers are added at the middle and near the base of the arrangement as color accents.

Arrangement:
With the potted scotch broom providing the basic form of the arrangement, the cut flowers are arranged at the middle and low positions to fill the flowerless space. Use larger cut flowers to balance with the small clusters of scotch broom flowers.

Spring 11

Materials:
Potted plant: Cineraria
Cut flowers: Marguerite, sweet pea
Outer container: Rattan basket

The potted cineraria, marguerite and sweet pea are arranged quite naturally in this composition.

Arrangement:
1 Place the cineraria in a fairly deep rattan basket. Prepare marguerite stems of various lengths so that they can add movement at all three positions. Prepare one stem of sweet pea flowers as a color accent.

2 Use the densely growing cineraria as the middle and low materials. Arrange the marguerite flowers at the high, middle and low positions, to nicely balance with the cineraria.

Space the marguerite flowers widely for a more attractive effect.

Spring 12

Materials:
Potted plant: Primrose
Cut flowers: Baby's breath,
   Dracaena fragrans 'massangeana'
Outer container: Plastic pot cover

This arrangement is composed of two parts. The right features the natural line of the materials, while the left is abstract in form.

Arrangement:
1 Place the potted primrose with its brilliant red flowers in a white container. White baby's breath and green dracaena leaves will accentuate the beauty of the primrose.

2 Arrange the two broad dracaena leaves vertically, to contrast with the natural lines of the primrose.

By having two different types of expressions in one composition, you add interest, while enhancing the beauty of each plant.

Summer 1

Materials:
Potted plant: African marigold
Cut flowers: Reeves spirea,
  anemone
Outer container: Ceramic pot

The low, densely growing potted African marigold is usually arranged as the middle material, but here it occupies the high position, with the flowing branches of the Reeves spirea set below it.

Arrangement:
Select a beautiful anemone flower to place in the center of the arrangement as a focal point of the composition. The Reeves spirea, which flows downward from both sides, gives a wonderful sense of movement to the arrangement. Arrange these branches with a slight imbalance between right and left, to improve the flow.

Summer 2

Materials:
Potted plant: Jasmine (*Stephanotis floribunda*)
Cut flowers: Elegant lily, statice
Outer container: Ceramic pot

This arrangement uses a potted jasmine, which has a vine-like quality, as the high material, with the statice and elegant lily integrated into it at the middle and low positions. It is important to vary the forms as well as the colors of your floral materials, and to achieve a desirable balance of strong and delicate flowers.

Arrangement:
The swaying tendrils of the jasmine stems add movement to the top of the arrangement, while the elegant lily and bunches of statice flowers lend stability by being integrated at the middle and low positions. Use both half-open and fully open lily blossoms for variety.

Summer 3

Materials:
Potted plant: Saintpaulia
Cut flowers: Freesia, sword fern
Outer container: Basket with a
  handle

This arrangement combines three completely different types of materials in a simple composition.

Arrangement:
1 Place the potted saintpaulia in a basket with a handle. Leave a large empty space between the low-blooming saintpaulia flowers and the basket handle. Arrange the freesia and the sword fern to fill the upper part of this space and to add movement to the composition.

2 To spotlight the interesting shape of the sword fern leaves, arrange them with the front of their leaves quite visible. Add two freesia flowers of varying heights and appearance. To make the delicate saintpaulia look more attractive, the added materials should be as simple as possible.

Summer 4

Materials:
Potted plant: Solomon's seal
Cut flowers: Bulrush, star lily,
  Campanula
Outer container: Ceramic pot

This arrangement uses a potted Solomon's seal after its flowers are gone, along with a small volume of bulrush, star lily and bellflower. By arranging these four very different materials appropriately in the high, middle and low positions, you can achieve an airy, refreshing effect.

Arrangement:
1 Since few leaves grow near the roots of the Solomon's seal, you should hide the base of the plant in a deep container. To emphasize the bountiful size of the container, use a minimal amount of cut flowers.
2 Spotlight the elegant lines of the bulrush by arranging one stalk tall and erect and bending the other in half. Remove some of the leaves of the star lily and arrange it at a high position.

Summer 5

Materials:
Potted plant: Fuchsia
Cut flowers: Chinese bellflower
Outer container: Bamboo basket

This combination of the luxuriant fuchsia and a bamboo basket gives a soft effect, but the addition of dramatic Chinese bellflowers, with their strong lines, more clearly defines the entire arrangement and gives it more impact.

Arrangement:
1 Because the fuchsia has a Japanese feeling, it goes nicely with a bamboo basket.
2 This densely growing potted fuchsia is well-balanced with the deep woven basket. The Chinese bellflowers add interest by disturbing the equilibrium, and they help unify the composition.

Summer 6

Materials:
Potted plant: Ivy geranium
Cut flower: Stokesia
Outer container: Glass vase

In this compact arrangement, ivy geranium and stokesia are unified by being placed in a cool white glass container.

Arrangement:

1 The main material in this arrangement is a potted ivy geranium, whose leafy green stems extend diagonally upwards to the left and right and whose flowers face in different directions at the upper and lower left. Because the flowers extend to the sides, you should use a small vase to make the flowers look larger.

2 Arrange three pink stokesia in the large empty space at the center of the ivy geranium at differing, but relatively low, heights. The pink flowers should be well-integrated into the green leaves of the ivy geranium to retain the line and express the characters of the materials.

Summer 7

Materials:
Potted plant: Hibiscus
Cut flowers: Japanese sasa lily, gladiolus, statice caspia
Outer container: Ceramic pot

This impressive potted hibiscus, with its lustrous green leaves and sparkling white blossoms that blush red deep within, complemented by tall Japanese lily, gladiolus and caspia flowers, form a strongly vertical composition. Because the hibiscus is the focus of the composition, distracting movement by the other flowers has been kept to a minimum.

Arrangement:
1 The low-growing potted hibiscus has dense leaves and has a flower that blooms near its base, for a low center of gravity. Place the Japanese sasa lily at a rather high position to maintain the balance of the arrangement.
2 Add the red gladiolus at the middle position as a color accent, but use just a small volume of flowers to avoid overpowering the other materials.

The caspia grass lends a gentle sense of movement.

Summer 8

Materials:
Potted plant: Caladium
Cut flower: Sunflower
Outer container: Ceramic pot

This is a very simple, summery arrangement combining a potted caladium, whose white leaves veined with green give a refreshingly cool impression, and sunflowers, the most representative of all summer flowers.

Arrangement:
1 The caladium leaves show a rich variety of expressions, depending on the angle from which they are viewed. When setting the pot into the container, carefully consider the angle from which the plant will look its best.
2 Use an equal amount of caladium leaves and sunflower stems at a high position. Try to achieve a delicate nuance by combining their colors and shapes.

Insert another sunflower to fill the space at the base of the arrangement and to unify the flowers and the container.

Summer 9

Materials:
Potted plant: *Dracaena sanderiana*
Cut flowers: Clematis, dendrobi-
  um orchid
Outer container: Bamboo basket

This is an ideal midsummer
arrangement using a potted dracaena, whose white-bordered
leaves give a fresh impression, a
vivid purple clematis flower
arranged at a high position, and
white dendrobium orchids near
the base.

Arrangement:
1 Allow the dracaena to be fully
visible in its middle section, to
highlight the beauty and movement of its leaves. In ikebana, it is
important to know when to omit,
as well as add, elements. Choose
an appropriate basket container
for that purpose.
2 Integrate a single clematis flower
at a high position to bring out the
beauty of the two plants. Twist
the vinelike clematis stem around
the dracaena branches.
  Add a small volume of dendrobium orchids near the base to
solidify the composition.

Autumn 1

Materials:

Potted plant: *Pachystachy lutea* Nees

Cut flowers: Japanese blueberry, small chrysanthemum

Outer container: Bamboo basket with a handle

This arrangement employs the large leaves of *pachystachy lutea* Nees, with its towering yellow flowers, at a high position, and small chrysanthemum and autumn-tinted Japanese blueberry branches at the middle and low positions. The extending Japanese blueberry branch adds flowing movement (*nagashi*) to the composition.

Arrangement:

1 Set the potted *pachystachy lutea* Nees into a bamboo container with a large rim and with a handle. Place the plant so as to show its upper leaves to their best advantage.

2 Arrange the Japanese blueberry branches at the middle and low positions, with one branch extending to the side and slanting slightly forward. The length of the branch should be less than the height of the arrangement.

Add the small chrysanthemum at the center in the middle position as a color accent.

103

Autumn 2

Materials:
Potted plant: Chrysanthemum
Cut flowers: False spirea,
  knotweed, foxtail millet
Outer container: Rattan basket

This arrangement consists solely
of autumn materials.

Arrangement:
1 To create an arrangement with
an autumnal atmosphere that
emphasizes the beauty of the
chrysanthemum flowers, include
simple wild flowers and grasses,
such as false spirea, foxtail millet
and knotweed.

2 Since the chrysanthemum leaves
lack visual appeal, conceal them by
arranging a mass of false spirea at
the middle and low positions.

Adding the foxtail millet at a
high position and the knotweed at
the middle position lightens the
effect of the overall composition.

Autumn 3

Materials:
Potted plant: *Chlorophytum comosum*
Cut flowers: Chinese bellflower
Outer container: Plastic container

This modestly sized arrangement consists of two pots of *chlorophytum comosum* placed in an oblong plastic container with white and purple bellflowers inserted near the container's mouth.

Arrangement:
1 Select an oblong container of adequate depth.
2 To display the beautifully variegated *chlorophytum comosum* leaves to their best advantage, integrate the bellflowers low into the leaves. Select one fully open bellflower, one half-open flower, and one bud for variety.

Autumn 4

Materials:
Potted plant: Indian lilac
Cut flowers: Wild nandina,
  lion tail
Outer container: Ceramic bowl

This arrangement uses a potted late flowering Indian lilac for the lower part. A small branch of wild nandina with colored leaves and seeds gives a feeling of autumn to the arrangement.

Arrangement:
1 Though Indian lilac naturally grows to be a tall plant, potted varieties are grown to be artificially small. Therefore arrange it deliberately low in a container which is itself low.

2 Wild nandina is also a tall plant, but to balance with the Indian lilac, use the short branches. In order to emphasize its beautiful colored leaves, try to create "flowing" movement with them.

By inserting three pieces of lion tail to form the upper part, this arrangement comes to symbolize a landscape of "an adjacent forest and distant mountains."

Autumn 5

Materials:
Potted plant: Chinese chili pepper
  (*Capsicum annum*)
Cut flowers: Chinese bellflower,
  giant reed, Gentian
Outer container: Ceramic bowl

This shows a typical arrangement consisting of upper, middle and lower parts.

Arrangement:
1 Using densely growing chili pepper for the lower part, three different autumn cut flowers are arranged to create the feeling of Japanese autumn. Choose cut flowers which bring out complete-

ly different feelings from each other.
2 Because bellflowers have a distinct outline, showing only a single flower at a middle position produces a better effect. If it is arranged with empty space in the background, its beauty is even more striking.

Insert a giant reed to form the upper part and to convey the image of blowing wind.

Autumn 6

Materials:
Potted plant: Basket plant
  (*Aeschynanthus*)
Cut flowers: False spirea, dahlia
Outer container: Hanging
  container

The basket plant has blossoms which resemble tubes of lipstick and beautifully thick, lustrous leaves. Since its vines hang downwards, this plant is best used for a hanging arrangement. In this composition, false spirea and dahlia are integrated into the basket plant leaves at the top as a color accent.

Arrangement:
1–2 Arrange the false spirea with its dense small white flowers at a high position, to highlight the rich green hues of the basket plant leaves.

Integrate the crimson dahlia into the false spirea and green leaves to create the focal point for the arrangement.

Autumn 7

Materials:
Potted plant: *Pilea cadierei*
Cut flowers: Toad lily, hardy
  begonia
Outer container: Bamboo basket

In this composition a potted pilea with densely growing green leaves is arranged in a roughly woven bamboo basket along with stems of toad lily and hardy begonia.

Arrangement:
1 Set the potted pilea so that the height of its leaves descends gradually from left to right.
2 Insert the toad lily at the back to fill spaces with sparse pilea leaves, especially from the center to the right, and integrate them with the pilea.

Arrange the hardy begonia at the base, thus creating a variation of the popular three-level composition of high, middle and low materials.

Autumn 8

Materials:
Potted plant: Maranta
Cut flowers: Finetooth holly,
  gentian
Outer container: Satchel or bag

This eye-catching arrangement
uses an overnight bag for the outer
container.

Arrangement:
1 Place a potted maranta with
beautifully veined leaves in a
satchel or bag of an appropriate
size. You can also adjust the
mouth with the zipper.
2 To highlight the beautiful pat-
terns of the maranta leaves,
arrange a modest volume of gentian. Insert the finetooth holly
branches at the front of the
arrangement for overall integration with the maranta leaves.

Autumn 9

Materials:
Potted plant: Saintpaulia
Cut flowers: Cockscomb, Chinese
   miscanthus (eulalia)
Outer container: Ceramic vase

The fully opened ears of the Chinese miscanthus tell us that autumn is fully upon us. In this example, the most representative of Japanese autumn plants, Chinese miscanthus and cockscombs, are combined with a potted saintpaulia. The outer container is a bright-blue ceramic vase consisting of two cone shapes, one upright and one inverted.

Arrangement:
1 Arrange the lovely pink potted saintpaulia so that it fully covers the container's mouth. The gentle effect of the pink blossoms and the sharply contoured blue container create an interesting contrast. Choose a saintpaulia laden with blossoms so that it can add weight to the lower part of the arrangement.
2 Insert two ears of Chinese miscanthus of varying heights at a high position. Use only the ear of the grass to heighten the feeling of late autumn.

Arrange the cockscomb at a middle position for an arrangement consisting of high, middle and lower materials.

Winter 1

Materials:
Potted plant: Croton (*Codiaeum variegatum* 'Akebono')
Cut flowers: Dendrobium orchid, rose, anthurium
Outer container: Fancy cookie tin

The croton has sharply outlined, multicolored leaves that are prominently displayed at a high position in this arrangement. By having one stem of anthurium dynamically extending outward, a sense of movement is given to the whole arrangement.

Arrangement:
1 Place the potted croton to one side of a fancy cookie tin.
2 Arrange the dendrobium orchids and the rose stems in the spaces among the lower croton leaves to stabilize the center of the arrangement.

Arrange one anthurium at a low position to consolidate the base and another extending outward for a sense of movement.

Part 4

Arrangements in Varied Containers

Materials:
Potted plant: Poinsettia
Cut flowers: Narcissus, baby's breath
Outer container: Rattan basket

Materials:
Potted plant: Saintpaulia
Cut flowers: Chrysanthemum
Outer container: Bamboo basket

Materials:
Potted plant: Primrose julian
Cut flowers: Pine, *Dendrobium phalaenopsis*
Outer container: Rattan basket

Materials:
Potted plant: Jasmine
Cut flowers: baby's breath,
  delphinium
Outer container: Basket

Materials:
Potted plant: Superb pink
Cut flowers: Sunflower
Outer container: Basket

Materials:
Potted plant: Duranta
Cut flowers: Elegant lily, scabiosa
Outer container: Bamboo basket

Materials:
Potted plant: White and red
  Riegers begonia
Cut flowers: New Zealand flax
Outer container: Basket

Materials:
Potted plant: Ivy geranium (*Pelargonium peltalum*)
Cut flowers: *Miyamayomena savatieri*
Outer container: Bamboo container

Materials:
Potted plant: *Kochia scorparia*
Cut flowers: Chinese miscanthus, Chinese bellflower, patrinia, tinted maple
Outer container: Bamboo basket

Materials:
Potted plant: Carnation, Cineraria
Cut flowers: *Asparagus myriocladus*
Outer container: Bamboo basket with a handle

Materials:
Potted plant: Bouvardia
Cut flowers: Willow, pine, sweet pea
Outer container: Bamboo basket

121

Materials:
Potted plant: *Thilandesia cinea*
Cut flowers: Clematis, bear grass
Outer container: Ceramic pot

Materials:
Potted plant: *Teika kadzura*
Cut flowers: Statice, mimosa
  acacia, jasmine
Outer container: Ceramic pot

Materials:
Potted plant: Boston fern
Cut flowers: Gentian, scabiosa,
  solidaster
Outer container: Ceramic pot

Materials:
Potted plant: Maidenhair fern
  (*Adiantum*)
Cut flowers: Ranunculus, freesia
Outer container: Ceramic pot

Materials:
Potted plant: *Culceoralia*
Cut flowers: Reeves spirea
Outer container: Tall ceramic pot

Materials:
Potted plant: Cyclamen
Cut flowers: Gerbera, baby's
  breath, narcissus
Outer container: Plastic pot cover

Materials:
Potted plant: Persian violet
  (*Exacum affine*)
Cut flowers: Water lily, statice,
  caspia, bulrush, amaryllis,
  · superb pink
Outer container: Glass bowl

Materials:
Potted plant: Christmas cactus
Cut flowers: Gerbera, nandina
Outer container: Ceramic pot

Materials:
Potted plant: *Philodendron xanadu*
Cut flowers: Elegant lily, baby's breath, delphinium
Outer container: Ceramic pot

Materials:
Potted plant: Zebra plant (*Calathea* sp.)
Cut flowers: Solidaster, lily
Outer container: Ceramic pot

Index of Plant Materials